Rivers of Fire

Rivers *of* Fire

The Story of Volcanoes

By Monica Halpern

NATIONAL GEOGRAPHIC

Washington D.C.

One of the world's largest nonprofit scientific and educational organizations, the National Geographic Society was founded in 1888 "for the increase and diffusion of geographic knowledge." Fulfilling this mission, the Society educates and inspires millions every day through its magazines, books, television programs, videos, maps and atlases, research grants, the National Geographic Bee, teacher workshops, and innovative classroom materials. The Society is supported through membership dues, charitable gifts, and income from the sale of its educational products. This support is vital to National Geographic's mission to increase global understanding and promote conservation of our planet through exploration, research, and education.

For more information, please call
1-800-NGS-LINE (647-5463) or write to the following address:
National Geographic Society
1145 17th Street N.W.
Washington, D.C. 20036-4688
U.S.A.

For information about special discounts for bulk purchases, please contact
National Geographic Books Special Sales at ngspecsales@ngs.org

Visit the Society's Web site: www.nationalgeographic.com

Library of Congress Cataloging-in-Publication Data

Halpern, Monica.
Rivers of fire : the story of volcanoes / by Monica Halpern.
p. cm. -- (National Geographic science chapters)
Includes index.
ISBN-13: 978-0-7922-5946-6 (library binding)
ISBN-10: 0-7922-5946-7 (library binding)
1. Volcanoes. 2. Volcanism. I. Title. II. Series.
QE522.H158 2006
551.21--dc22

2006016332

Photo Credits
Front Cover: © Digital Vision/ Getty Images; Spine: © Digital Vision/ Getty Images; Endpaper: © Digital Vision/ Getty Images; 2-3: © Tui De Roy/ Auscape; 6: © Maurice & Katia Krafft/ Auscape; 8: courtesy U.S. Geological Survey; 9: © Maurice & Katia Krafft/ Auscape; 11: © Robert W. Madden/ National Geographic Image Collection; 12: © Digital Vision/ Getty Images; 14: © Bates Littlehales/ National Geographic Image Collection; 15: © Nature Picture Library; 16: © Tui De Roy/ Auscape; 17 (left): © Timothy G. Laman. National Geograohic Image Collection; 17 (right): © ANT Photo Library; 18: Maurice & Katia Krafft/ Auscape; 22-23: © Reuters/ Corbis; 24: © Photolibrary.com; 26: © Bettmann/ Corbis; 27: © Charles O'Rear/ Corbis; 29: © Photolibrary.com; 30: © P. Bourseiller-HoaQui/ Auscape; 32-33: © Maurice & Katia Krafft/ Auscape; 34: © Getty Images; Illustrations by Dimitrios Prokopis.

Contents

The erupting Mount St. Helens threw a huge cloud of ash thousands of feet into the air.

On the Scene at Mount St. Helens

Sunday, May 18, 1980

It is a bright, sunny morning on Mount St. Helens. Deep green forests cover its slopes. The snowcapped mountain shines in the sun. Below, a crystal clear lake sparkles.

Then, at 8:32 a.m., there is a tremendous explosion. People in nearby towns are knocked off their feet. The air fills with a big cloud of gas, ash, and steam. The sky turns black in an instant.

The blast is so loud that people 200 miles (322 km) away hear it. The sky is dark for more than 250 miles (402 km).

No one should have been surprised by this blast. Scientists knew it was coming. In March, the mountain had began to send out a little steam and ash. Then, a bulge grew on one side of the mountain. The bulge grew bigger and bigger. By mid-May, it looked like a huge blister about to pop.

Scientists kept a watchful eye on the bulge growing on the side of Mount St. Helens.

This car was buried under the ash that blew
from Mount St. Helens.

It wasn't the first time that Mount St.
Helens had exploded. Native Americans
who have lived in the Cascade Mountains
for a long time call Mount St. Helens "Fire
Mountain." It has blown up five times in the
last 280 years. The last time was in 1857.

Monday, May 19, 1980

The mountain sends out red-hot rock and
steaming mud. It throws rocks high into the
air. The hot ash and burning rocks melt the
snow. A boiling river of mud races down the
mountain. It destroys everything in its path.

Hot winds blow as hard as winds during a hurricane. They knock down forests. The flattened trees look like matchsticks. Every living thing in the forest is dead.

The air is still thick with dust and ash. People have to wear face masks to protect their lungs.

Sunday, May 25, 1980

In the morning, another smaller blast takes place. The sky is dark with ash and smoke again. The street lights come on in some places even though it is morning.

Gray ash covers everything. People are shoveling it out of the streets. Some towns are using snowplows to clear the ash away. The land looks like pictures of the moon. Will anything ever grow here again?

The towns near Mount St. Helens were covered in a cloud of ash and smoke after the eruption.

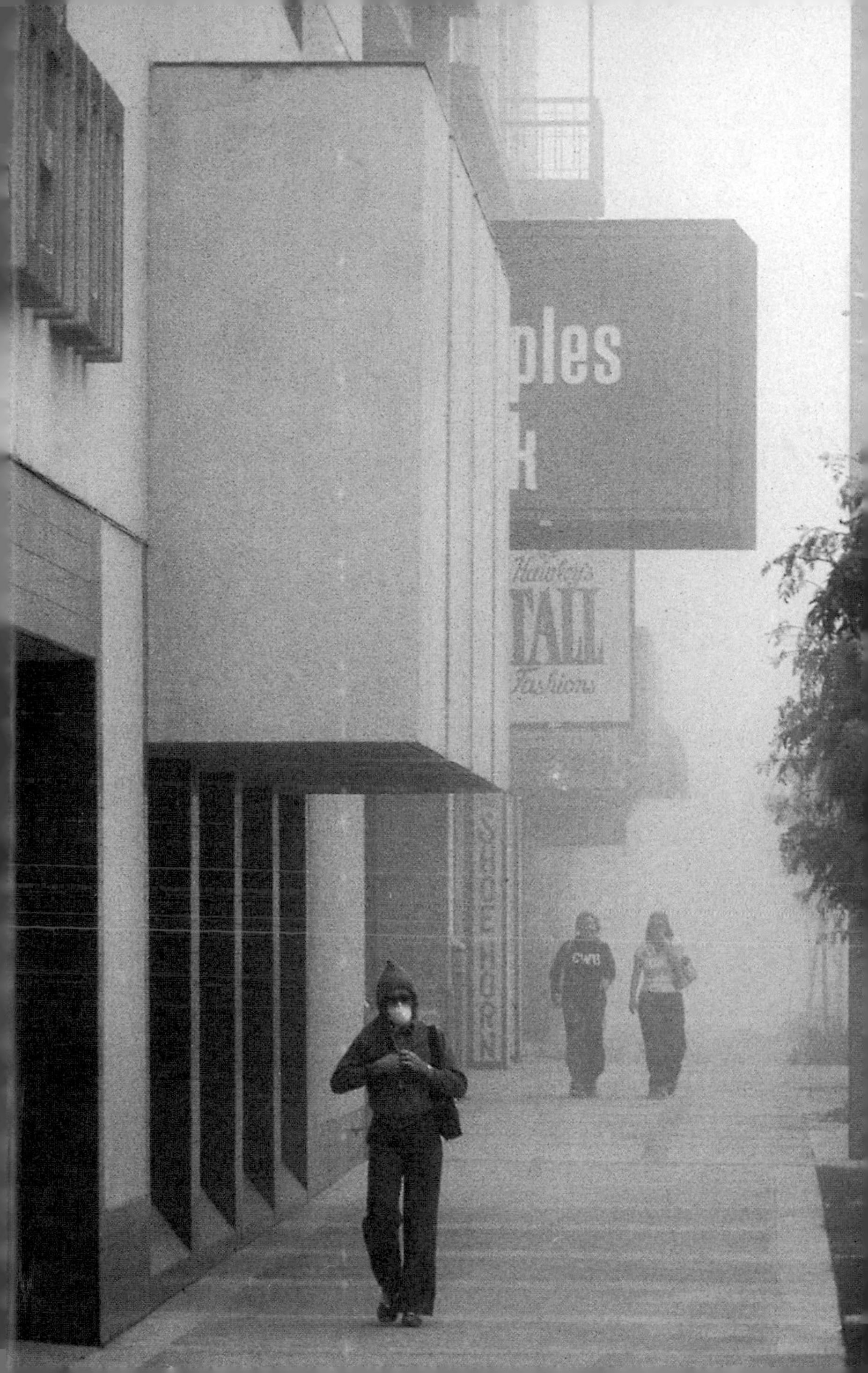
ples
Hawley's
TALL
Fashions
SHOE HORN

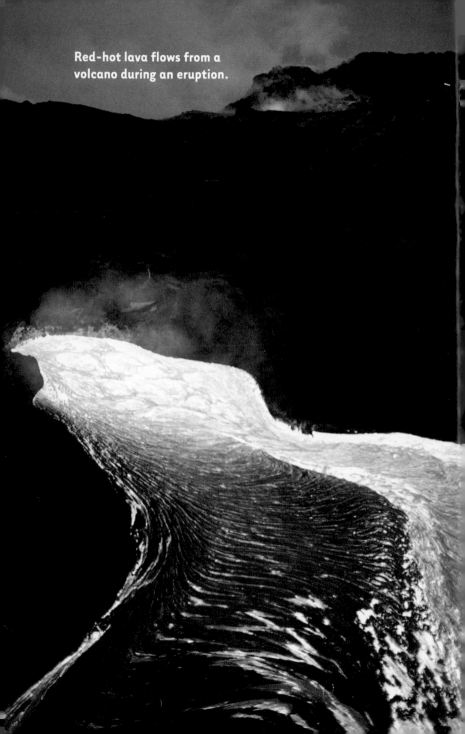
Red-hot lava flows from a volcano during an eruption.

Chapter 1

What Are Volcanoes?

Volcanoes are powerful. They can be very destructive. But what are they and how do they form?

A volcano is an opening in the surface of Earth out of which melted rock and gases sometimes explode. The word *volcano* refers to the mountain that builds up around this opening. Picture fire gushing out of the top of a mountain. That's what a volcano can look like when it explodes.

How Volcanoes Form

Earth is made up of different layers. The thin outer layer is Earth's crust. Below the

crust is a hot, thick layer of rock. It's called
the mantle. Some of the mantle is so hot that
its rocks have melted. They have turned into
a liquid called magma. Below the mantle is
the core.

Imagine a steaming, bubbling soup of
magma, deep under the surface of Earth.
The Earth's crust is not perfectly solid.
There are cracks in it. Sometimes, magma

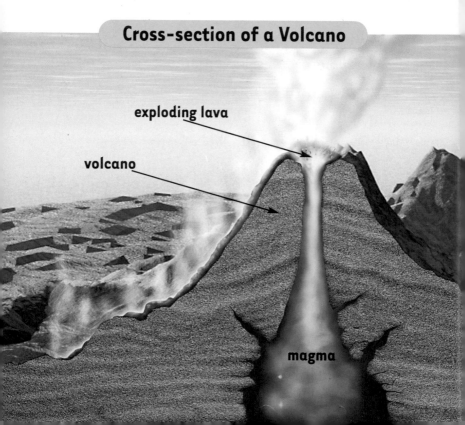

Cross-section of a Volcano

exploding lava

volcano

magma

bursts through one of these cracks. A volcano is formed. Hot liquid rock, called lava, explodes into the air.

Mount St. Helens is a volcano that formed long ago. But once a volcano has formed, another eruption is likely to take place there some day.

A shield volcano erupts on one of the Galapagos Islands in Ecuador.

Types of Volcanoes

Volcanoes come in three different shapes. A shield volcano is wider than it is high. It is large and rounded. A composite volcano looks like a tall mountain. Its peak has steep sides. But its sides are often flatter near its base. It's made up of mixed layers of cinders and lava. A cinder cone is a cone-shaped hill. It is much smaller than a shield or a composite volcano, but it has very steep sides.

Volcanoes erupt in different ways. Like Mount St. Helens, some volcanoes explode violently. They blow out hot rocks and ash at over 300 miles (483 km) per hour. These volcanoes usually have steep sides.

Some volcanoes erupt more gently. These volcanoes produce a runny lava that oozes out and flows down its side. These volcanoes usually spread out over a wide area. They are low and round.

▲ This volcano in Hawaii is a cinder cone.

◄ Mount Fuji, in Japan, is a composite volcano.

Chapter 2

Where Are Volcanoes Located?

Volcanoes do not occur everywhere. Some places on Earth have a lot of volcanoes. Other places have none.

Earth's crust is broken up into big slabs of rock called plates. These plates move around very slowly. Sometimes, the plates push together or pull apart. When that happens, magma can move up between the plates, forming a volcano. Most volcanoes happen at the edges of plates.

Some volcanoes lie far away from the edges of plates. These places are known as

Mauna Loa, in Hawaii, is in a hot spot.

"hot spots." Here, Earth's crust is very thin. Magma rises up and bursts through the crust. It forms new volcanoes. Some lie under the ocean. Some happen on land. But others have burst out of the ocean to form new islands. The Hawaiian Islands were formed this way.

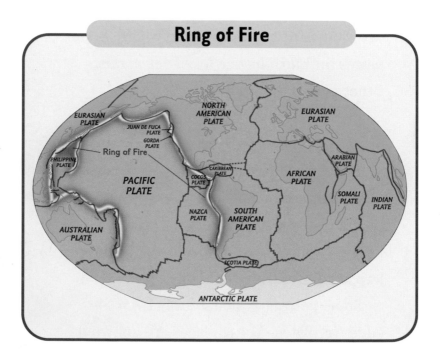

Ring of Fire

So many volcanoes form around the Pacific plate that the area is called the "Ring of Fire."

Some volcanoes are quiet for a long time. They still show signs of life, such as steam rising. Scientists call these volcanoes dormant, which means "sleeping." The volcanoes may erupt again in the future.

If a volcano shows no signs of life for a very long time, it is called extinct. Scientists believe that it has stopped erupting. There are about 500 active volcanoes in the world. Only 10 to 20 of these active volcanoes erupt each year.

People Who Study Volcanoes

Scientists who study volcanoes are called volcanologists. These scientists watch how volcanoes act. They also study old rocks and hardened layers of ash from eruptions that happened long ago. From these clues, they can figure out how many times a volcano has erupted.

In 1978, two scientists found that Mount St. Helens was one of the volcanoes in the

United States most likely to erupt. They
predicted that the volcano might erupt
before the year 2000. They were right. Two
years later, Mount St. Helens blew up.

Today, scientists are able to predict fairly
well when a volcano will erupt. By watching
a volcano, they learn to recognize the
warnings it gives before erupting. They use
several kinds of information to make their

A volcanologist wears a special suit to study volcanoes up close. The suit protects the volcanologist from the heat.

predictions. They measure any gases escaping from it. They look for any bulges. They measure the movements of the plates. Small earthquakes near a volcano may mean that an explosion is near.

But no two volcanoes are alike. They act in different ways. A volcano may give many warning signs but never erupt. Other volcanoes erupt without warning.

You can see Mount Vesuvius
through this arch.

Chapter 3

Volcanoes in History

Mount St. Helens is a famous volcano of today, but it is just one of many famous volcanoes throughout history.

Mount Vesuvius

Mount Vesuvius erupted in Italy in the year A.D. 79. It completely buried the nearby city of Pompeii in more than 18 feet (6 m) of ash. As time passed, Pompeii was forgotten. The ruins of Pompeii were rediscovered in the 1700s. People worked to uncover the town. They found coins, jewels, and statues. They even found the remains of meals that were left when the volcano erupted.

Today you can still see the position people were in when Mount Vesuvius blew nearly 2,000 years ago.

The rain of hot ash killed many people. Over time, the bodies decayed, leaving hollow shells of hardened ash. Scientists filled these holes with plaster. Then they chipped the hardened ash away. They were able to see what the people looked like.

Today you can visit the ruins of Pompeii. It is like a city frozen in time. Pompeii shows how powerful and destructive a volcano can be.

Krakatau

Another huge disaster was caused by Krakatau. This island volcano in Indonesia blew up in 1883. Some say that the noise of the explosion was the loudest sound ever made. People as far away as 3,000 miles (4,800 km) heard the explosion.

Krakatau became two islands in the eruption of 1883.

The explosion blew the island in half. It also caused enormous waves 120 feet (37 m) high. No one was living on Krakatau. But the waves crashed onto nearby islands where many people lived. More than 36,000 people were swept away.

Waves from Krakatau spread around the world. They hit the coasts of England and France. They hit North and South America. A dust cloud 50 miles (80 km) high traveled around the world.

Famous Volcanoes

Year	Volcano	Place	Estimated Deaths
79	Vesuvius	Italy	16,000
1586	Kelud	Indonesia	10,000
1669	Etna	Italy	20,000
1792	Unzen	Japan	15,000
1815	Tambora	Indonesia	90,000
1883	Krakatau	Indonesia	36,000
1902	Pelée	Martinique	30,000
1985	Nevada del Ruiz	Colombia	23,000

Anak Krakatau is a smaller island volcano that was formed after one of Krakatau's explosions.

Chapter 4

After a Volcano Erupts

Besides destroying property and killing plants, animals and people, volcanic eruptions can also change the world's weather. A cloud of ash from an eruption can climb more than 7 miles (12 km) high. some of the ash can stay in the air for more than two years. It can block the sunlight.

Mount Tambora in Indonesia erupted in 1815. In 1816, spring and summer all over the world were cold. People called it the year without a summer. Crops died and many people went hungry.

◀ The village of Pinatubo, in the Philippines, was covered in volcanic ash in 1991.

Volcanoes can be useful, too. Everything may look gray and lifeless after a volcano has blown. But old lava makes very good soil for farming. The lava has many minerals that are good for plants.

The rocks, lava, and other things thrown out by volcanoes have other uses, too. Some are used as building materials. Others are used in cleaning products.

People have found valuable gems and metals around old volcanoes. They have discovered some big diamonds, as well as sapphires. Miners have found copper, silver, and gold in old volcanoes, too.

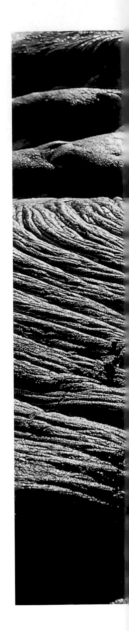

New plants grow out of the old lava.

Returning to Mount St. Helens

After Mount St. Helens erupted, it was a gray and lifeless place. But after a few years, green plants began to grow. Flowers bloomed. Insects came to pollinate the flowers. Birds came back to eat the insects. Of course, there are no tall trees. It will take many years for the forests to grow back.

Mount St. Helen's is still an active volcano. Scientists watch it carefully. They think it will blow up again some day. But that day will probably not come for a long time.

New plants and wildlife began to appear at Mount St. Helens in the years following the eruption.

How to Write an A+ Report

1. Choose a topic.

- Find something that interests you.

- Make sure it is not too big or too small.

2. Find sources.

- Ask your librarian for help.

- Use many different sources: books, magazine articles, and websites.

3. Gather information.

- Take notes. Write down the big ideas and interesting details.

- Use your own words.

4. Organize information.

- Sort your notes into groups that make sense.

- Make an outline. Put your groups of notes in the order you want to write your report.

5. Write your report.

- Write an introduction that tells what the report is about.

- Use your outline and notes as you write to make sure you say everything you want to say in the order you want to say it.

- Write an ending that tells about your report.

- Write a title.

6. Revise and edit your report.

- Read your report to make sure it makes sense.

- Read it again to check spelling, punctuation, and grammar.

7. Hand in your report!

Glossary

cinder cone a type of volcano that looks like a cone-shaped hill

composite volcano a type of volcano that is made of layers of cinders and lava and looks like a tall mountain with steep sides

core the thick center of the earth

crust the thin outer layer of the earth

dormant having a time without activity, such as a volcano that is not erupting

erupt to pour or explode out of an opening

extinct no longer alive or active, such as a volcano that scientists think will not erupt in the future

lava hot melted rock on Earth's surface

magma hot melted rock beneath Earth's crust

mantle the thick middle layer of Earth between the crust and the core

plates big slabs of rock that make up Earth's crust

shield volcano a type of volcano with a rounded shape that is wider than it is high

volcano an opening in Earth out of which melted rock and gases sometimes erupt

volcanologist scientist who studies volcanoes

Further Reading

• Books •

Grace, Catherine O'Neill. *Forces of Nature: The Awesome Power of Volcanoes, Earthquakes, and Tornadoes.* Washington, D.C.: National Geographic Society, 2004. Ages 9-12, 64 pages.

Lauber, Patricia. *Volcano: The Eruption and Healing of Mount St. Helens.* New York, NY: Aladdin, 1993. Ages 4-8, 64 pages.

Omeara, Donna. *Into the Volcano.* New York, NY: Kids Can Press, 2005. Ages 8-12, 56 pages.

Stamper, Judith. *The Magic School Bus: Voyage to the Volcano.* New York, NY: Scholastic, 2003. Ages 4-8, 96 pages.

Tanaka, Shelley. *The Buried City of Pompeii: What It Was like When Vesuvius Exploded.* New York, NY: Hyperion, 2000. Ages 12 and up, 48 pages.

Van Rose, Susanna. *Volcanoes and Earthquakes.* New York, NY: DK Publishing, 2004. Ages 9-12, 72 pages.

• Websites •

CyberSleuth Kids
http://cybersleuth-kids.com/
sleuth/Science/Earth_Science/
Volcanoes/

Federal Emergency Management Agency (FEMA)
http://www.fema.gov/kids/
volcano.htm

How Volcanoes Work
http://www.geology.sdsu.edu/
how_volcanoes_work/Home.
html

The Kids Research Center
http://www.gigglepotz.com/
krc_volcanoes.htm

National Geographic Society
http://www.nationalgeographic.
com/ngkids/0312/

Science News for Kids
http://www.sciencenewsforkids.
org/articles/20041222/Feature1.
asp

Time for Kids
http://www.timeforkids.com/
TFK/specials/articles/
0,6709,202270,00.html

Index

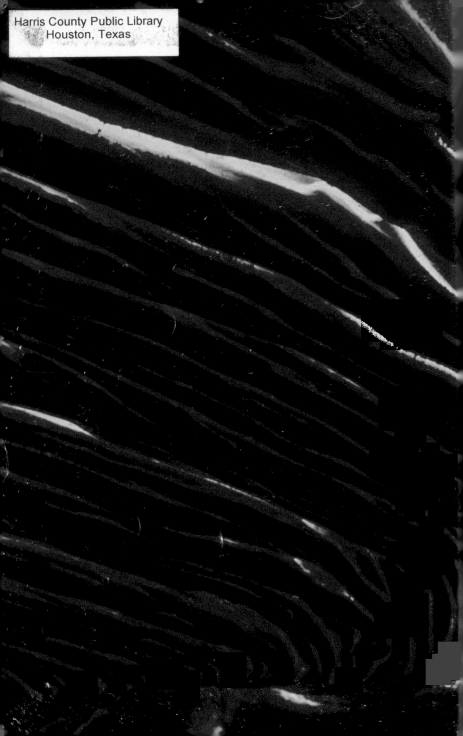